My Mersey Tale: Keep Your Eyes Open, Look Up When Possible...

By Stephen Guy

FATHER and son got off the train to start another adventure exploring an unfamiliar location offering new sights and sounds.

During the 1920s Roger Bolland Guy liked to make the most of his precious leisure time. He and wife May had nine children and it was often a struggle making ends meet at their home in Hamilton Road, Everton.

Roger liked to take his youngest son George on walks away from the bustling family home.

Roger was an introspective man who would get keyed up with the stresses and strains of life. Walking in peace and quiet was an antidote.

On this occasion they left Roby station and explored the leafy lanes and pretty cottages before taking a path over Childwall Valley. The only sounds were the harsh calls of corncrakes and trilling of skylarks.

The footpath meandered uphill to Childwall Church where father and son opened the gates on Score Lane before "reaching civilisation", as granddad put it, at Wavertree and the tram home.

I inherited a love of exploring the environment as George, my father, would take me walking virtually from the time I could stand up.

He disapproved of cars and walked whenever possible right up to his death, aged 87.

There is no better way of getting to know a place than exploring at a walking pace. Buildings, paths, roads, rivers and streams all tell stories in some form or another. My father would bring places to life by telling

stories linked to places we saw. It might be a disaster or national event or some local mishap that electrified the local community long ago. This brought out an appreciation of architecture, age of buildings and their functions.

Both my mother and her mum Lillian Potter, an active member of the Independent Labour Party, were excellent storytellers. As well as telling new anecdotes gleaned from daily events, they could bring the past to life – rare gifts.

Merseyside Tales started appearing in Saturday's Liverpool ECHO back in 2011 and this book contains some of my favourites, plus a new article about Lowlands, the Grade II-listed West Derby Community Centre, where I am a director.

The tales reflect my deep interest in history. I won prizes for getting top results in both History O-level and A-level at Evered High School in Walton.

When I became a news reporter with the Echo, and later Press Association (the national news agency), my knowledge of history and the way it is presented was very helpful in my work.

It was when I joined National Museums Liverpool as press officer that I came to appreciate the similarities between journalists and exhibition curators – they both tell stories or narratives.

The tales draw on my own interests and material I have gathered and inherited over the years – books, pictures, diaries and letters. Almost anything can inspire a tale

and I like to put historical events into contemporary contexts.

It is not just the built environment – buildings would be nothing without people. People bring stones, bricks and mortar to life. There are very many people who have helped make Liverpool into the present day major world city – King John, William Roscoe and Gladstone immediately spring to mind.

There are countless others, from talented business people and shipowners to entertainers and sports personalities.

Merseyside's former administrative role was objectionable to some local people but the topographical area reflects the scope of the tales.

Merseyside traditionally includes places near or on the banks of the River Mersey. Most of the tales have a Liverpool focus with forays into neighbouring satellite areas and further afield.

I suppose one message of this book is to keep your eyes open. It's a cliché but look up whenever possible, particularly in Liverpool city centre, as there are unnoticed architectural gems everywhere.

It's also rewarding to look at people. One sunny lunchtime I was amazed to see Hollywood star Bette Davis out alone exploring Liverpool city centre. Another time I spotted one of my favourite stars, Kenneth More, crossing Lime Street. In a Southport café I heard a familiar voice, turned around and saw Brief Encounter star Trevor Howard eating a fry-up.

EARLY DAYS

A strategically important port, Liverpool was
swept up in civil unrest and bitter fighting

Burning Beacons

BEACONS were used to spread news of danger quickly and effectively – there are references to them in ancient Persia, Palestine and Greece. In the Bible, Jeremiah called on the people of Benjamin to make a fire signal on a mountain.

Beacons were used both by day and night – a smoking fire was just as visible as flames in the dark.

A 1455 Scottish Act of Parliament enshrined in law the types of beacons to be used when the English were invading. One bale of blazing straw indicated they were on their way, while four meant a great army was on the march.

Everton Beacon stood overlooking Liverpool for centuries. The 30ft high structure was made of local sandstone and was probably built when England was threatened by the Spanish Armada in 1588.

Similar beacons were erected throughout England so news of the Spanish fleet could be passed on rapidly. The Pope had told Philip II of Spain that he could have Protestant England and the king set out to oust Elizabeth I. He assembled an armada of 130 large ships carrying 20,000 soldiers. England had a fleet of just 30 small vessels.

In the event, the panic-stricken Spaniards fled after the English sent fire ships into the Armada. The Spanish tried to get away by sailing north around Scotland pursued by the English.

Some Spanish ships were captured, but many were wrecked in storms and just 53 made it back to Spain.

If the Spanish fleet had approached Liverpool, the 18ft square, two-storey Everton Beacon would have swiftly linked up with other beacons at Billinge, Ashurst and Black Combe in Cumberland.

Everton Beacon was kept in good repair until the middle of the 18th century, by which time new forms of signalling and communication had been developed. It became dilapidated and squatters moved in. An old cobbler was the last resident in about 1783. Finally, Everton Beacon fell down during a storm in 1803.

The beacon was replaced by a wooden signal station nearby – this time to warn of a possible French invasion. In 1813, St George's Church was built on the site of the beacon, at a cost of £11,500, by public subscription.

SIGNAL STATION

St George's Church which replaced Everton Beacon

Families at War

IT was 1424 and Liverpool was swept up in the Wars of the Roses bringing civil unrest for almost a century before ending when the Tudors took the throne.

The port was dominated by two wealthy, powerful families – the Molyneuxes in Liverpool Castle and the Stanleys in Liverpool Tower.

These two fortresses dominated the waterfront and all manner of plotting and political intrigue must have gone on within their walls.

The Wars of the Roses involved a power-struggle between two Royal dynasties – the Houses of Lancaster and York. The conflicts started in 1399 when warrior Henry IV of Lancaster seized the throne from weak but brave Richard II, the last Plantagenet king.

For decades, the wars were largely political before erupting into 30 years of armed conflict culminating in the Battle of Bosworth in 1485, when Richard III was killed and Henry Tudor became Henry VII. Peace came and England prospered.

In 1424, Liverpool experienced what was to become common in the wars that swept the land – two great families fell out but, fortunately, a battle involving thousands of armed men was narrowly avoided on the intervention of the king.

The rival Molyneuxes and Stanleys were usually political allies connected by marriage but were jealous of each other's power and influence.

In the heat of midsummer, an argument flared up between Sir Richard Molyneux and Thomas Stanley. Supporters of both factions gathered in Liverpool. It is not known exactly what caused the row, but it became so serious that Henry VI intervened.

Thomas rallied more than 2,000 men in the belief that he was about to be attacked by Sir Richard's supporters. The King's sheriffs seized Thomas and then went looking for Sir Richard who was marching with 1,000 armed men across West Derby fen towards Liverpool. Sir Richard was also arrested and Henry banished the two belligerents to Windsor and Kenilworth Castle to cool off.

Liverpool Castle was built around 1235 and for hundreds of years was the largest building in the town. It gradually fell into disuse and the last remnants were removed in 1726.

Liverpool Tower as a stronghold dated from 1406 and it stayed in the possession of the Stanleys on and off until 1702. Ironically, in 1648, during the Civil War the daughters of the Earl of Derby were imprisoned there and later Lord Molyneux in 1651.

At one time it was a place of grand entertainment but ended up serving as Liverpool Jail as well as assembly rooms for dancing, cards and other jollities.

The Tower was pulled down in 1819 when Water Street was widened and Tower Buildings stand on the site.

STRONGHOLD
Liverpool Tower depicted during a storm

Under Siege

THE English Civil War saw the King pitched against Parliament in a fight to the death over two conflicting philosophies – a monarch chosen by God and a Government elected by the people.

Liverpool, as a strategically important port on the Irish Sea, was the scene of bitter fighting and suffered three sieges in 18 months.

Charles I believed in the Divine Right of Kings and tried to rule without Parliament, which was dominated by the Puritans.

Their brand of austere Christianity was despised by most of the aristocracy who made up the Royalist faction. The Puritans – dubbed Roundheads – wore simple clothing contrasting with the flamboyant fashions of the Royalist Cavaliers. The first siege took place in May 1643, when the Royalists fought for two days before capitulating to the Roundheads.

Local grandee Colonel John Moore held Liverpool as governor for Parliament. The King sent his dashing nephew Prince Rupert to recapture the port in the second siege in June 1644.

The haughty prince pitched camp in Everton overlooking his target. He used a humble hovel as his headquarters – it was forever afterwards known as Prince Rupert's Cottage.

His army had carried out a massacre in Bolton and Rupert's arrival struck terror into the people of Liverpool. Many women and children were ferried across the Mersey to Storeton, Wirral, where they were guarded by the Roundheads.

About 400 people died in the hand-to-hand fighting as Rupert's soldiers fought their way into Liverpool to successfully retake the heavily fortified town. John Moore fled by sailing up the Lancashire coast.

A 19th century artist showed Rupert's siege under way with plumes of smoke billowing over the port dominated by its ancient castle. Ships lie at anchor on the river and in the Pool.

Sir Robert Byron was holding Liverpool for the Royalists when the third siege began in September 1644. A Roundhead force led by Sir John Meldrum bombarded the town for two months.

Finally, the Royalist defenders had enough and mutinied before deserting to Sir John. Liverpool was in Roundhead hands for the rest of the war.

Moore returned as governor but was criticised for fleeing – it was said he wanted to save his extensive property in the town including his residence, Bank Hall. He was replaced as governor by hardliner Lt Col John Ashurst in May 1645.

The port took on a new significance as an important embarkation point for troops sailing to Ireland, where the bloody fighting continued into the early 1650s.

Roundhead leader Oliver Cromwell had a string of successes and won the war – Charles I was beheaded. England was a republic until the restoration of the monarchy in 1660.

BATTLE GROUND

Above, Prince Rupert's cottage. Below, the earliest
known view of Liverpool, dated 1680. Left, a
drawing of Liverpool at the time it was besieged

HISTORIC HARBOUR

Liverpool waterfront with castle. The castle saw virtually no military action throughout its five centuries of history. Inset, St George's Church, built on the site of the castle, lasted from 1734 until its demolition in 1899, where the Victoria Monument now stands

King of Castles

LIVERPOOL Castle dominated the town for nearly 500 years, standing on a rocky outcrop overlooking the Pool.

For centuries, it was the largest building in the port, protecting the inhabitants from invasion or disorder. The fortress was built around 1235 by William de Ferrers, after Liverpool was granted its first Charter by King John in 1207.

Four massive towers gave the castle an imposing presence, although it saw virtually no military action in its long history.

William Herdman made a drawing of Liverpool Castle from an etching of 1780. It shows the riverfront with a section of Liverpool Tower to the left.

The castle had been held by the Molyneux family (later Earls of Sefton) and the Tower occupied by the Stanleys (Earls of Derby).

The building with the door in the centre, with a horse and cart in front, is Liverpool's third Custom House. The first was a thatched building in High Street and the second in Moor Street.

By 1559, Liverpool Castle was described as being decayed and ruinous. It saw a new lease of life in the Civil War but after that fell into decay once more.

It became an increasing embarrassment and in 1704 the Corporation successfully applied to lease the site from the Crown and demolish the castle.

This was eventually done about 1725 and St George's Church was built on the site, opening in 1734.

The church is pictured in 1792 after it had become a prominent landmark. It was said to stand on the site of the castle's chapel. The church stood on a raised plateau, the remains of the outcrop of rock on which the fortress had stood.

A series of vaults were hewn in the rock – here many leading citizens were buried. The church also had secular uses. One of the two octagonal buildings at the corners was used by the clerk of the markets and the other as a lock-up for troublemakers.

St George's was designed by Thomas Steers, who created the Old Dock at the mouth of the Pool.

The church tower was built partly on the site of the old castle moat. The landfill settled over the years and the spire had to be taken down in 1809.

Ten years later, the church was reconstructed in what was considered an inferior style.

St George's was demolished in 1899 and the Victoria Monument built on the site.

The long-gone obelisk mounted with an ornamental lamp was put up by John Tarleton, who was Liverpool's Mayor in 1764.

A short street called Castle Hill, opposite the end of Moor Street, reminds us of this vanished age.

HAY DAYS

Childwall tithe barn. Left, the original Tudor tithe barn, in Tithebarn Street, Liverpool. Bottom left, haymaking in Stoneycroft in 1909

Era of Barn Barons

IT WAS 1524 and powerful Liverpool baron Sir William Molyneux decided to build a tithe barn in the fledgling port. The family had been prominent in the area for more than 400 years. His ancestor, William de Moulines, distinguished himself in the Battle of Hastings, helping William the Conqueror take England from the Saxons.

The Molyneuxes acquired increasing wealth and power as the centuries rolled by, effectively owning Liverpool with their great rivals, the Stanleys.

Henry VIII was on the throne and England grew in power and prestige as the century progressed. However, Liverpool remained largely unaffected at this period – her time would come with the growth of the British Empire.

For now, Liverpool was a tiny port of just seven streets clustered around the castle overlooking the Pool, a seaweed-filled creek that gave the place its name. The surrounding area was agricultural

with most people eking a living from the land. Sir Richard chose Moor Street, one of Liverpool's original seven byways (not to confused with the later road behind James Street).

Tithes were levies usually paid on crops and other agricultural produce. They were paid in kind, stored in buildings known as tithe barns.

The Liverpool tithe barn became a familiar landmark, so much so that Moor Street was soon renamed Tithebarn Street.

Originally, tithes were paid to the church, but as time went on some were sold, often to secure even more wealth for the great monasteries that flourished in the countryside.

The Molyneux family bought the living and tithes of Walton from Shrewsbury Abbey in Edward IV's time during the previous century.

The barn stood on the south side of Tithebarn Street at the corner of Dig Lane, later gentrified to Cheapside. After being disposed of by the Molyneuxes, the barn housed shops

and businesses. A bowling green was created at the back.

Celebrated Liverpool artist William Herdman drew the dilapidated but romantic building, which was partly demolished around 1820 for road widening. The rest was cleared many years later.

Outlying villages around Liverpool, including West Derby and Childwall, also had tithe barns which remained until about 100 years ago.

Liverpool had many rural aspects until fairly recent times. Haymakers were pictured off Black Horse Lane, Stoneycroft (now Queens Drive) in 1909.

Up to the 1960s, there were farms and small holdings in the outer suburbs, but they were gradually developed, largely to meet housing needs. The morning crowing of a cockerel was a familiar sound to me as a child in West Derby.

Today, there are few working farms left within the city boundary – probably the biggest is Home Farm, at Croxteth Hall.

PORT OF PROSPERITY

A boom in trade, transport and fashion, and a gruesome tale from the gallows...

SUPREMACY ON THE WAVES
Liverpool from Perch Rock at
the end of the 18th century

Privateer Lives

THE French vessel was triumphantly brought into the Mersey after being captured by a Liverpool privateer.

With the Carnatic safely moored in port, a thorough search was made of the East-Indiaman. Among her cargo was found a box brimming with diamonds, making this the richest prize of its kind.

It was 1779 and the value of the ship and cargo was an astonishing £135,000 – more than £10 million in today's money. This was the official figure, but some say the true value of the treasure ship was £400,000 (£30 million).

Britain was fighting for supremacy on the waves and privateers – privately-owned armed ships – were commissioned for war service by the Government.

This form of legalised piracy was seen as legitimate support for the Royal Navy.

The 400-ton Mentor, commanded by Captain John Dawson, was just one of around 120 privateers operating out of Liverpool.

She was not an obvious choice for such work, said to be clumsy and lopsided, but was knocked into shape and came up trumps.

Bristling with 28 guns and crewed by 102 men, she engaged and seized the unarmed Carnatic. Captain Dawson and Peter Baker, the owner of the Mentor, used part of the plunder to buy a country estate in Mossley Hill and built a mansion that became known as Carnatic Hall. The original Elmswood Road house was burnt down in Victorian times but was rebuilt and occupied by William Holland of the Lamport and Holt shipping line.

Other notable Liverpool privateers were Fortunatus Wright and William Hutchinson.

Captain Wright was a clever and intrepid adventurer. However, Captain Hutchinson – Wright's former first mate – was even smarter. He developed privateering as a science and recorded his strategies and tactics in a book called A Treatise on Practical Seamanship, published in 1777.

This was read by many budding privateers and may have helped in the capture of the Carnatic.

It was not only captains and ship owners who benefited from the spoils. In 1777, 13 Liverpool seamen each received £1,800 (about £130,000 today) as their share in prize money.

On the other hand, the cost of the war with France was high, with Britain losing more than 560 ships. As a result, goods such as tobacco, oil and pig-iron imported from America rocketed in price.

Privateer crews were known as hard men who committed many outrages when in Liverpool, often bringing terror to the town.

Local people sometimes took the law into their own hands – a mob looted the captured French prize L'Equité stranded off New Ferry.

Carnatic Hall was demolished in 1964 and the site developed as Liverpool University halls of residence, with the name preserved.

CONQUEST
The Mentor (right) captures
the treasure-laden Carnatic

Portrait of a Lady

TWELVE leading ladies of fashion were judged by their personal attributes in a mischievous article in the Morning Post newspaper read by the aristocracy and gentry.

One of the 12 was Isabella, Countess of Sefton, who lived at Croxteth Hall, Liverpool.

The Morning Post marked each lady out of 20. Lady Sefton scored 16 for her figure and 14 for her beauty – but only four for sense and just three for wit.

The article was probably a publicity stunt on behalf of Lady Sefton's younger sister Amelia, Countess of Barrymore, who scored 17 or more in each category!

The story is revealed by Alex Kidson in his fascinating new book, Earlier British Paintings in the Walker Art Gallery and Sudley House (Liverpool University Press / National Museums Liverpool, £35).

The 357- page hardback is lavishly illustrated with fact- filled narratives about the well- known as well as more obscure works in the two popular galleries.

A full-length portrait of Lady Isabella was painted by Thomas Gainsborough in 1769, shortly after her marriage. She wears a stunning white silk dress decorated with light blue and black stripes and a matching overdress.

It is likely that Lady Isabella never wore this costume, which was probably kept in the artist's studio. Gainsborough may have painted her face and hands from life separately.

An identical dress appears in a portrait of Lady Bolton, painted about the same time.

In 1777, Georgiana, Duchess of Devonshire, described Lady Isabella as "a compound of vanity, nonsense folly and good nature – for tho' many people deny her the last qualification I am sure she possesses it only she always contrives to put her faults in the clearest light".

Isabella (1748 – 1819) was the daughter of the Earl of Harrington. In the 1770s, her family name was given to urban development on land in south Liverpool owned by Lord Sefton.

The name is also remembered in Harrington Street, off Castle Street, in the city centre.

Gainsborough may have selected the portrait as one of his four exhibits at the Royal Academy inaugural exhibition in 1769 because the sitter was a person of fashion.

However, it was intriguingly called Portrait of a Lady to preserve Lady Isabella's anonymity – a failed strategy because she was recognised immediately.

The painting has subsequently gained a reputation as the epitome of Gainsborough's art of the late 1760s. It hung at Croxteth Hall for more than 200 years and was saved from a fire by quick- thinking staff in 1952.

When Isabella's descendant Hugh, last Earl of Sefton, died in 1972, it was accepted in lieu of death duties and transferred to the Walker in 1975.

PICTURE PERFECT

Croxteth Hall Isabella, Countess of Sefton, in a Gainsborough portrait now hanging in the Walker Art Gallery. Left, Croxteth Hall

GRIM GALLOWS

The two windmills were renamed Gallows Mill after the gruesome executions of four prisoners found guilty of high treason. Inset, King George I

Jacobite Rebellion

THE rebellion had failed and the prisoners were rounded up to be tried in Liverpool and other parts of the country.

Britain was divided by the claims of James Edward Stuart who assembled an army in his attempt to reclaim the crown as James III.

His father, the Catholic convert James II, has been ousted in the 1688 Glorious Revolution by the Protestant William of Orange who defeated the King at the Battle of the Boyne.

It was now 1715 and James – later known as the Old Pretender because of his claim to the throne – saw his chance. William of Orange had married James' half-sister Mary but the couple died without children. James's other half-sister Anne succeeded to the throne. However, none of her 17 children survived childhood.

Under the Act of Settlement 1701 banning Catholics from the throne, German Prince George Louis – the Elector of Hanover – became King George I of England in 1714.

The Earl of Mar led James' supporters – known as Jacobites – but the insurrection was a miserable failure with the rebels surrendering at Preston.

Two of the leaders – the Earl of Derwentwater and Lord Kenmure – were taken to London and beheaded on Tower Hill. Others escaped.

Whole towns had turned out in favour of the Stuarts, including Warrington where most of the inhabitants thronged in their Sunday best to celebrate James' birthday as church bells pealed. Similar scenes were witnessed in Manchester.

However, Liverpool was deeply loyal to George and prepared fortifications to protect the town. Up to 160 captured Jacobites were put on trial before three judges. A total of 34 people were executed for high treason in Liverpool, Preston, Garstang, Wigan, Lancaster and Manchester.

The four Liverpool executions took place at the edge of the town in a field at the top of London Road, to the east of what is now Stafford Street.

Two nearby windmills were called the Gallows Mills following the gruesome executions – the prisoners were hanged, their bodies cut into four pieces and their heads put on spikes.

Some of those convicted at the trials were members of the landed gentry including Richard Chorley, head of an ancient Lancashire family. Others were transported from Liverpool to plantations in the colonies.

Some 130 were shipped abroad at a cost of £1,000.

One group of prisoners heading for the West Indies from Liverpool overpowered the captain and crew and sailed to safety in a French port.

The Government paid Liverpool compensation for the fortification work which was spent on building St George's church.

The Jacobites attempted another unsuccessful invasion in 1745 led by James' son, Bonnie Prince Charlie.

GOING LOCO

Rainhill. Below, two images of early locos with their carriages – the Jupiter and the North Star

Age of Steam

THE excitement had been building up for months following the Rainhill Trials – the Liverpool to Manchester Railway was at last a reality. Steam engines had been developing slowly over the decades but it took the genius and vision of George Stephenson to build and successfully launch the revolutionary form of transport.

Until steam locomotives, the pace of land travel had been dictated by the speed of a horse. Before roads were improved in the 18th century, travel was slow, uncomfortable and dangerous.

Things started to change in 1750 when the gambling Earl of March wagered that a four-wheeled carriage could travel 19 miles in one hour.

He won his 1,000 guinea wager by building a special lightweight carriage pulled by four horses which raced over Newmarket Heath in the record time.

Speed was now the focus of engineers and entrepreneurs as Britain grew more and more prosperous: they wanted to shift people and goods as quickly and cheaply as possible.

The reality of the new age came with the Rainhill Trials in October 1829 when Stephenson's Rocket beat off rivals to win the competition. Backers now knew their plans for the railway would no longer be just a dream.

Rainhill (pictured about 100 years ago) will forever be synonymous with the Rocket and railways. Today, train travel has spread throughout the world, but when the Liverpool to Manchester Railway opened in September 1830 some people viewed it with trepidation.

The trains could travel at more than 30mph – twice as fast as the best mail coaches. The Ship Inn at Rainhill was the first coach stop out of Liverpool where horses were changed – there was stabling for about 140 animals.

Now the train had come and some people feared that they would suffocate if they travelled at, for the time, fast speeds.

Once the trains started to run regularly such fears vanished. The construction of the line had been fraught with difficulties – the vast Chat Moss peat bog was one of the obstacles to be overcome.

At first, train services from Liverpool started at Edge Hill because of the huge works needed to cut through the solid rock to the centre of Liverpool.

There are still lots of reminders of those early days – for example, the original stone bridges and the Lion locomotive on display at the new Museum of Liverpool.

Cusp of Greatness

THE members of Liverpool Corporation stared in amazement at the ancient painting of their town. It was 1818 and they could hardly believe that their large, important port could have grown from such a small community in less than 140 years.

The oil painting depicted Liverpool in 1680, when a castle dominated the fledgling port. The town had seen little growth in hundreds of years, but things were about to change dramatically.

The painting was presented to the town by Ralph Peters, whose family had owned it for many years. His grandfather had been Liverpool's town clerk from 1707 to 1743.

Liverpool in 1680, possibly by a Dutch artist and now in Merseyside Maritime Museum, is the earliest known authentic depiction of the port. It shows St Nicholas' parish church, Liverpool Tower, original town hall and castle in fascinating detail.

The only thoroughfare distinctly shown is Water Street leading down to the shore where ships were beached to be unloaded – this was 35 years before the first dock was built.

The river is bustling with vessels of all shapes and sizes. Warships fly huge ensigns and bristle with cannons. Merchant ships prepare to unload valuable cargoes. Tiny rowing boats bob on the waves.

Liverpool was starting to see spectacular growth linked to the burgeoning British Empire. Canny business people saw the potential of trade with the growing American colonies and invested in the port.

Liverpool had overtaken Chester in terms of shipping and crews. Just three decades before this picture was painted, Chester had 15 vessels totalling 383 tons crewed by 63 men, while Liverpool had 24 ships totalling 462 tons with 76 men.

By 1689, Chester had no more than 20 ships of between 20 and 60 tons, while Liverpool had up to 70 ships of between 50 and 200 tons each.

About 100 years ago, W Fergusson Irvine produced a map showing Liverpool in 1668 from contemporary records – no original map of the town exists from that date.

Roughly 5,000 people lived in Liverpool at this time shortly after Charles II came to the throne.

The original seven streets can be seen – Water Street, Dale Street, Chapel Street, Tithebarn Street, Castle Street, Old Hall Street and Juggler Street (now High Street). Several later roads, such as Fenwick Street and Moor Street, are depicted.

The Pool – the creek that gave the town its name – is crossed by two bridges. The Townsend Bridge stands at the end of Dale Street, crossing over what is now Byrom Street.

The wooden Pool Bridge spans present day Paradise Street to the unnamed road leading to the heath (later Duke Street).

CHANGING TIMES

'Liverpool in 1680', the earliest known view of the port. Above, W Fergusson Irvine's plan of Liverpool in 1668

MAYOR
Richard Gildart painted in 1768

POST HASTE
Umpire coach travelling
between Liverpool and London

Ride into History

HORSEDRAWN coaches clattered into town carrying bundles of eagerly-awaited letters in a period of sustained growth which saw Liverpool begin to mushroom in size.

A coach service between the port and London had been established by 1766 as improved roads enabled coaches to travel relatively quickly.

For centuries, roads were often largely impassable because they were poorly maintained. Huge potholes created hazards. In wet weather, the highways became quagmires, while dry conditions turned them into dust bowls.

The first edition of Gore's Liverpool Directory in 1766 reported regular coach journeys to the capital. It took two days in the summer but three in winter.

One travelled from the Golden Talbot Inn, Water Street, and the other from the Millstone in Castle Street. There were also coaches to other towns such as Manchester.

In January 1768, the Liverpool Chronicle reported an accident involving the driver of the Manchester coach. Around this time the comings and goings of the coaches had a particular interest for my great-great-great-great-grandfather Peter Guy (1736 – 1791).

He was Liverpool's only postman between 1769 and 1775 and had his work cut out. By 1770, Liverpool's population had risen to more than 34,000, so he would have been kept busy delivering, although some people collected their letters.

Peter must have known everyone of importance in Liverpool at this time. However, most people did not receive letters – many could not read or write.

Among his customers must have been Richard Gildart, the former mayor, who is depicted in a stunning portrait by Wright of Derby in the Walker Art Gallery's collection. It was painted in 1768 when the sitter was 95. He died in 1770.

Family tree research by my brother David has revealed more information about our ancestor.

Peter, one of five children, had also been a mariner and tidesman – a type of policeman who guarded ships awaiting inspections by Customs.

We like to think Peter helped bring about change. According to Victorian historian Sir James Picton, in 1773 the names of Liverpool's streets were first inscribed on the walls and the houses numbered.

This would have made Peter's job much easier. Before that he had to memorise addresses or ask locally.

Things were obviously getting too much for him because in 1775 Liverpool's inhabitants applied for more postmen.

The Post Office declined because only one letter-carrier was allowed in English towns. Presumably, this was for reasons of cost and security.

The post-coach Umpire, above, is pictured about 1820. It left Liverpool at 1pm every day and arrived at London's Charing Cross by 7pm the following day, so only one night was spent on the road.

Pottery Pride

THE breezy, bracken-covered Great Heath covered the hillside overlooking the Pool, the edge of the town. Liverpool was growing in importance when Samuel Shaw set up his pottery works between nearby Fontenoy Street and Trueman Street.

Business boomed and he extended his workshops on to the Heath – probably the first development in that area. Samuel's son Thomas was even more successful and took an active part in civic life as an alderman and mayor.

The area around the works was developed with houses, taverns and other premises. It was called Shaw's Brow after Thomas and became a densely populated part of the town by the 1770s. At this time, when my ancestor Peter Guy was Liverpool's postman, houses were numbered and street nameplates put up for the first time.

Thomas, who died in 1779, was a clever potter and his products were among the finest when Liverpool produced many different types of ceramics.

The most famous of all the Liverpool potters was Richard Chaffers, who was apprenticed

SHAW'S BROW

North Side. Below, South side,
featuring St George's Hall

to Thomas Shaw. Richard set up
a factory in Shaw's Brow with
moulding houses in Islington.

Like many people at the time, he
died young – just 34.

Seth Pennington carried on the
business and was famous for his
punch bowls, usually with shipping
subjects painted in blue.

Other potters on Shaw's Brow
included Philip Christian, who

produced high quality porcelain.

Shaw's Brow retained its rural
aspect on the edge of the town for
many years. A Mr Parker had a
commercial well, selling water at 9d
(3.5p) a butt.

His advertisement in a 1758
newspaper gushed: "The water is
soft and most excellent for washing,
and boiling peas."

Shaw's Brow declined as the

decades passed. Liverpool's
pottery industry shrank and finally
disappeared as the port boomed and
land was needed for other purposes.

The north side of Shaw's Brow is
seen in 1855 shortly before work
started on what is now the World
Museum. Demolition work can be
seen in the foreground.

The buildings on the south side
are depicted in a drawing from
1849. At that time, St John's Church
was crowded in by long terraces of
property. The terraces were cleared
away in 1855 and the street widened,
with some land being added to
St John's Churchyard (now
Gardens). Partly-built St George's
Hall symbolises the future.

By this time, Shaw's Brow was
rundown but still a bustling part
of the town. My great-grandfather
Henry Guy lived in Clayton Street at
the back of Shaw's Brow.

Between 1855 and 1906, Shaw's
Brow – renamed William Brown
Street – was swept away and
replaced by the great classical
buildings of today's Cultural
Quarter.

VICTORIAN CHANGE

A period of peace and prosperity saw the population boom as science and education led the way

The Sailors' Rest

LIVERPOOl, as second port in the British Empire, saw huge numbers of seafarers coming and going as ships arrived and departed.

In Victorian times, vessels often stayed in dock for several days as cargoes were loaded and unloaded.

Crew members came from all over the world with spare cash to spend in the town, particularly after a long voyage. Big ports had sailor towns where mariners could relax.

The Liverpool waterfront featured colourful taverns and bars where the tars were welcomed with open arms.

All crewmen knew to keep their wits about them because all manner of tricksters and unscrupulous rogues were out to make a quick buck at their expense.

A seafarer had to be able to use his fists as well as his brains if he was not to be cheated out of hard-earned cash.

The Liverpool Sailors' Home was an attempt by the authorities to make life easier for visiting crews.

Standing at the foot of Hanover Street, at first sight it looked more like a turreted Tudor palace, rather than cheap lodgings. A view looking towards the river by eminent Liverpool artist William Herdman shows the Home shortly after it opened in 1850. The effect is rather spoilt by clusters of shabby buildings which were later demolished.

A group of Liverpool citizens backed the idea of building safe, secure accommodation to improve the lives of seamen and keep them away from corrupting influences. These included crimps (swindlers), loan sharks, thieves and pick-pockets.

Prince Albert laid the foundation stone on July 31, 1846 – a commemorative medal was issued showing his portrait on one side and a view of the Home on the other.

Designed by John Cunningham, the £25,000 building featured a 70ft high central hall surrounded by cosy sleeping cabins – one is preserved in the collections of National Museums Liverpool.

The Home also had some facilities available to non-seafarers of the time – complete with bathrooms. Guests could take the sea air on a rooftop promenade and there was a library and concert hall as well as everyday facilities such as dining rooms, a bank and laundry.

I remember the Home well as a strange but atmospheric landmark when it had become outmoded and obsolete.

It closed in 1969, following a drop in demand, due to dock developments away from the city centre.

Cash could not be raised to modernise or find a new role for the building and it was demolished in 1974. Bits of masonry remained on the site until Liverpool One was developed.

Happily, the magnificent iron gates were returned in 2011 and stand on the site of the Home.

MEDAL MEMORY

Above, the medal that was struck to commemorate the opening of the Home. Right, the old Sailors' Home gates, now reinstated on the old site. Opposite page, the Sailors' Home pictured circa 1970

SAILORS' HOME

PATRIOT PUPILS

Bluecoat pupils on a St George's Day march. Top, the Bluecoat Arts Centre as it stands today

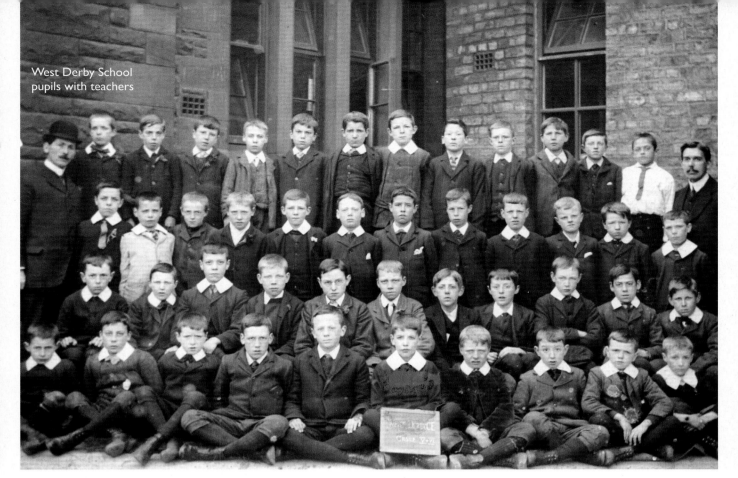

West Derby School
pupils with teachers

School's Out

PUPILS at a Liverpool school shared their tiny classroom with a cock, two hens and three terriers – the noise of the children, the cackling of fowls and the barking of dogs was deafening.

This was reported by officials compiling a six-month survey of the town's education establishments in 1835. It was the era when Charles Dickens created Dotheboys Hall, run by tyrannical headmaster Wackford Squeers in Nicholas Nickleby, a novel based on disturbing reality.

The Liverpool researchers put the schools into four categories, serving the town's total population at that time of 230,000. All charged fees.

Poor boys and girls attended 244 Dame Schools, named because most were run by older women in their homes. This ancient form of education, soon to be swept away by Victorian reforms, gave only basic instruction.

About 5,500 Liverpool children went to 194 Common Day Schools. There were about 50 Charity Schools such as the Bluecoat, first established in 1708, and the School for the Blind (1791).

Finally, around 4,000 middle-class children attended 143 private day or boarding schools.

Most schools for poor children left a great deal to be desired. Many of the Dame Schools were no more than miserable hovels with so-called lessons held in attics and cellars.

The researchers found a school with just one desk for 38 pupils. Only six of the scholars had a book.

Pupils at the charity and private schools fared much better. A contemporary illustration shows smartly-dressed pupils marching out of the familiar Bluecoat building in School Lane on St George's Day 1843. They are watched by admiring dignitaries such as the Mayor as well as townsfolk.

Shipowner Bryan Blundell helped establish the famous school after seeing the plight of poor children who often had to look after themselves once their parents died or abandoned them.

Liverpool Institute, dating from 1835, was to become one of Liverpool's most famous schools.

It started as the Mechanics' Institution, where workers could take evening classes. Boys were enrolled for the day school. There were 786 pupils by 1839, when it was decided to extend the building.

Country children perhaps had better conditions. Woolton was outside Liverpool at this time and was served with a stone-built school.

The simple building bears the date 1610. Over the door is the inscription, carved in Victorian times: "Much Woolton Old School The Oldest Elementary School Building In Lancashire".

It ceased to be a school about 1860.

Legislation from 1870 transformed education, gradually introducing universal schooling. By the time pupils at West Derby Church of England School were photographed around 1900, Britain's education system had vastly improved.

Skull for
Scandal

CRUEL KILLER

Dr William Palmer, and a letter he
sent to his wife, one of his alleged
victims in his murderous spree

CLOSE TO 30,000 people crowded outside the jail to watch
the grim spectacle – some of the better-off paid a guinea
(£1.05) to sit in comfortable grandstands.

There was a murmur of anticipation as the accused man climbed
the ladder up to the scaffold. Dr William Palmer declared his
innocence as the hangman, dressed in a top hat and long white
coat, adjusted the rope before sending him to eternity.

It was June 14, 1856, and among the throng was a scientist who
had travelled from Liverpool to Stafford Prison with a specific task.

Mr Bridges, of the Phrenological Institute, 30, Mount Pleasant,
later joined officials crowded around Palmer's body.

Bridges carefully examined Palmer's head before making a
plaster cast. He declared that the head revealed Palmer was "a
criminal type of the worst character", as the Liverpool Daily Post
reported.

The case had been a sensation which had rocked Rugeley,
Staffordshire, to its foundations. The citizens of the little town were
so upset that they vainly tried to get the place renamed.

Cold and calculating but with a boyish charm, Palmer ruthlessly
despatched anyone who got in his way.

He poisoned his victims and the motive was often money. His
own family were not immune – Palmer would give his babies a
comforting finger laced with honey and poison to suck. Alleged
victims included his wife, mother-in-law, brother, uncle and at
least one of the children he had by 14 girls around the town, as
well as legitimate offspring.

Although from an affluent family, he racked up huge debts from
gambling. Many of his other victims were murdered to clear debts.
Palmer thought himself immune as he was a doctor and came from
a respectable family – one brother was a vicar, another a solicitor
and his charitable sisters did good works.

Doubtless the cast of Palmer's head was excitely interpreted
back in Liverpool. Phrenology was a branch of science concerned
with the function of the human brain. Now largely discredited,
it relied on assessing the shapes and sizes of skulls. The
expression that someone "needs their bumps feeling" refers
to phrenology. The Victorians were strong believers in its
accuracy.

Palmer's father owned a sawmill and left more than
£40,000 when he died in 1830. The family had Liverpool
connections. Palmer's brother, Joseph, served his
apprenticeship with a timber merchant in the port.
However, William Palmer did not have a
successful time in Liverpool. After leaving school
at 16, he was apprenticed to a wholesale druggist
in the town but was dismissed after being
caught stealing.

Returning to Rugeley, he was apprenticed
to a surgeon and eventually qualified as a
doctor in London.

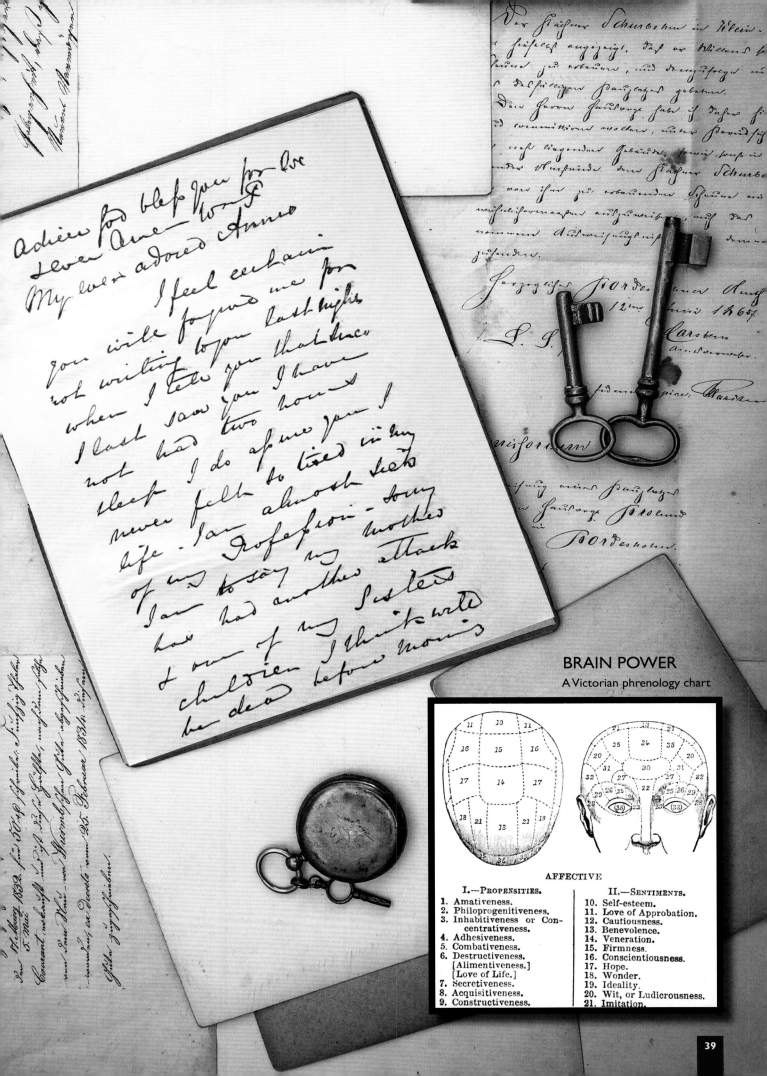

BRAIN POWER
A Victorian phrenology chart

AFFECTIVE

I.—PROPENSITIES.
1. Amativeness.
2. Philoprogenitiveness.
3. Inhabitiveness or Concentrativeness.
4. Adhesiveness.
5. Combativeness.
6. Destructiveness.
   [Alimentiveness.]
   [Love of Life.]
7. Secretiveness.
8. Acquisitiveness.
9. Constructiveness.

II.—SENTIMENTS.
10. Self-esteem.
11. Love of Approbation.
12. Cautiousness.
13. Benevolence.
14. Veneration.
15. Firmness.
16. Conscientiousness.
17. Hope.
18. Wonder.
19. Ideality.
20. Wit, or Ludicrousness.
21. Imitation.

Steam Leader

BRITAIN was under threat of invasion by French emperor Napoleon III and Liverpool people prepared to defend the port.

A thousand men marched down Water Street, led by charismatic shipowner Col Charles MacIver, who had drilled and trained the soldiers.

It was 1858, and this was one of the first volunteer regiments to be raised. Liverpool suffered during the long war with Napoleon III's uncle, Napoleon Bonaparte, and needed to be prepared.

This new threat of invasion fizzled out. As well as being a pioneer of the volunteer soldier movement, MacIver helped spearhead the growth of steamships.

He was a business partner of Samuel Cunard, whose vision and enterprise transformed shipping in the Victorian era.

MacIver was the dominant shipowner in Liverpool between 1850 and 1880. He was a striking figure. In an age when virtually all men – apart from the clergy – sported whiskers, MacIver was clean-shaven.

With his aquiline features and firm mouth, he appeared born to command. MacIver's personal and professional courage was well-known.

He could also ruthlessly maintain discipline and be unkind by today's standards.

One of his captains once asked to take his wife on a voyage. MacIver agreed, but, on the day of sailing, the captain was handed passenger tickets for himself and his wife but was replaced by someone else as ship's commander.

As his prosperity grew, MacIver lived in bigger and better houses to reflect his status. He resided in Canning Street and Abercromby Square before moving to Dovecot House (now Dovecot Park). In 1873, he settled in his final Liverpool home – the Mansion House in Calderstones Park.

MacIver lived there until 1881 when he moved to Malta, probably for his health. The estate remained in his family until being acquired by Liverpool Corporation as a public park, opening in 1905.

It remains one of the city's most popular recreation areas. The lake was built in 1933 as part of a job creation scheme during a period of high unemployment.

I have many happy memories, including visiting the mansion when it was open to the public and contained many portraits and paintings.

My father did a watercolour of the house in 1978, including the popular greenhouses, which were demolished some years ago. The air was laden with the scent of exotic plants and flowers – each glasshouse got hotter and hotter as you walked through.

Cunard is known throughout the world today, but it is unlikely he would have achieved such success without the skills of colleagues such as Charles MacIver.

The MacIver link with the Cunard Line continued for many years. A later chairman of Cunard, Sir Percy Bates, married MacIver's granddaughter.

HISTORIC HOME

Calderstones mansion and greenhouses, as depicted in a watercolour in 1978. Above, Liverpool steamships owner Colonel Charles MacIver

Off to Market

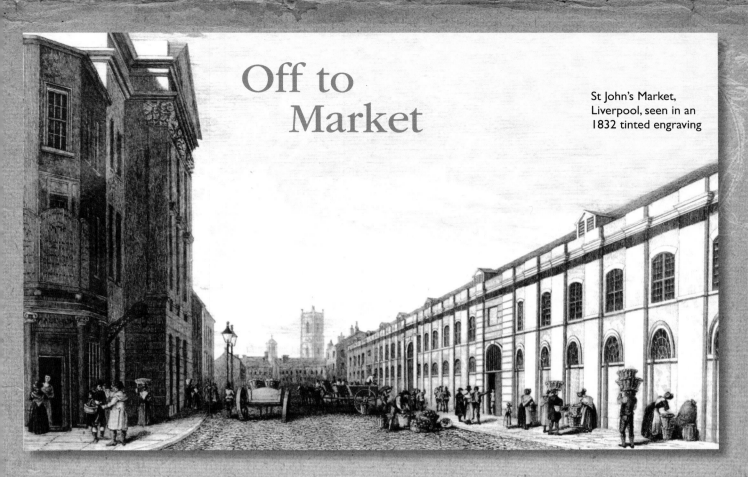

St John's Market, Liverpool, seen in an 1832 tinted engraving

THE ruined fortress, which dominated the town for centuries, was being demolished to create much-needed space.

Liverpool Castle symbolised the old port created by King John in 1207, principally as a departure point for armies sailing to Ireland. By 1700, Liverpool was growing as a major commercial centre where trade drove economic growth. Many citizens were growing in wealth and prosperity and needed somewhere central to buy and sell. They saw the castle as an ideal town centre market site.

For generations, Liverpudlians made do with pitching stalls in narrow streets – butchers traded from shambles off High Street, near the present Town Hall.

Corn was sold at the High Cross, where piles of grain stood in the street and a potato market was spread around the nearby White Cross.

From 1702, land was cleared around the castle for trading, although some of the ruins remained. Ancient walls were torn down in 1721 to accommodate the growing market in newly-named Derby Square. The rest of the castle was pulled down about five years later.

Other markets sprang up but, a century after its creation, the Derby Square market had mushroomed and become overcrowded.

On Wednesdays and Saturdays, stalls and booths extended along Castle Street almost to the Town Hall. There were many complaints from shopkeepers and the public. This led to the creation of St John's Market in 1822, creating a permanent trading centre under one roof.

Once the market moved, the area around Derby Square and Castle Street acquired its current character as a commercial centre.

St John's Market is seen in an 1832 tinted engraving. Carts are unloaded in Great Charlotte Street – many would have come from farms around the town. Several people carry baskets on their heads. On the left is the Amphitheatre (later replaced by the Royal Court) with St Luke's Church in the distance.

I remember the original St John's Market very well, with its vast hall crammed with all manner of goods. I have particularly fond memories of the fascinating old streets clustered around the market. Shawled women known as Mary Ellens sold fresh cucumbers from straw baskets.

A musty second-hand bookshop invited entry. Over the road stood a pet shop and a cart with puppies in tiny cages. All this was swept away around 1964 to be replaced by today's St John's Centre, with its modern market and shops.

The 450ft high St John's Beacon became a major landmark and is seen here shortly after completion in 1971 looking up Cases Street. This view vanished when the Clayton Square development was built over the far end of the street.

TIME OFF

ↄ৵

Holidaymakers flocked to golden beach resorts, while the arrival of a daredevil star caused a stir in the sky

The New Brighton Tower and
Red Noses sandstone crags

Pretty as a Postcard

THE holidaymaker was enjoying his stay at New Brighton and chose a colourful postcard to send to a friend in Yorkshire.

It was the Whitsuntide weekend of 1913 and an AC wrote to Janet in Huddersfield: "Frank and the girls have played on the sands while Dad and I have been to the top of the tower. We have also seen the ship called Mauretania sail for New York."

It must have been a marvellous sight to see the great liners and other vessels from the lofty heights of New Brighton Tower. The Cunard Line's Mauretania and her doomed sister Lusitania were very popular on the Mersey.

Big crowds would gather on the shoreline to catch a glimpse of these leviathans loaded with passengers travelling to and from America.

New Brighton was a great vantage point and the Tower the best grandstand of all. Queues would form for a trip to the top – particularly at high tide when the big ships were coming and going at the quaysides.

Like the Lusitania, New Brighton Tower had a short life. Work began on its construction in 1896, at about the time the promenade was being built. The 562ft high Tower opened in 1900 and at was slightly higher than Blackpool Tower, which could be seen on a clear day on the other side of Liverpool Bay.

It was a big attraction in New Brighton, which was thronged with day trippers and people staying in the many hotels and boarding houses that filled the resort.

The postcard sent by AC to Janet shows the Tower at the peak of its popularity, with the Tower Ballroom at its base and gondolas on the lake. At this time, the Tower grounds boasted an amusement park featuring a bandstand and athletics ground with cycling and running tracks.

The ferry called at New Brighton Pier and visitors were spoilt for choice with so many attractions. The Tower was the focal point, but oases like Vale Park and the Red Noses scenic sandstone crags attracted those wanting a quieter time away from the hustle and bustle.

The Tower closed to the public at the outbreak of the First World War in 1914. It was neglected during the conflict and demolished in 1919, four years after Lusitania was torpedoed and sunk off Ireland with great loss of life.

New Brighton continued to be very popular for many decades until the advent of mass motoring and package holidays abroad saw people going elsewhere. The Tower Ballroom was a big attraction right up to the 1960s, when it hosted performances by The Beatles and many other groups of the time.

Old Duke's Folly

THE innkeeper decided to build a bathing house among the windswept sandhills to cash in on the new craze for plunging into sea water as an aid to health and wellbeing.

It was 1792 and William Sutton, who ran a tavern in Churchtown (then called North Meols), saw possibilities in the desolate coastline as a resort for the wealthy.

People were becoming more aware of the benefits of fresh air.

Britain's growing prosperity brought with it a desire to enjoy natural amenities – at about this time the first tourists were exploring the Lake District and the Prince of Wales made Brighton a fashionable retreat.

Sutton – known as the Old Duke – soon replaced his humble bathing house with a hotel grandly called the South Port Hotel, presumably because it was south of the River Ribble. Locals may have dubbed Sutton's establishment Duke's Folly, but a village soon sprang up around the hotel, forming the fledgling Southport.

Some people took in paying guests and the popular resort we know today came into being.

Postcards from about 1910 show Lord Street with surrounding landmarks – such as the Cheshire Lines station, Opera House and Winter Gardens marked – and Eastbank Street, where a horse-drawn cart follows tramlines

BUSTLING

Eastbank Street, Southport

outside the premises of Dent the brushmaker.

It was the railway that brought prosperity to Southport, when lines allowed people to commute from Liverpool and even Manchester as well as bringing holidaymakers from more distant places.

The Liverpool line opened in 1848 – in 1904 it became one of the first electrified routes in the country. The Manchester line followed around 1855.

The Cheshire Lines service started in 1884 and linked up with Aintree before eventually closing in 1952.

As its name suggests, the Southport Visiter once carried lists of people visiting the resort, a handy guide to who was in town.

I worked as a reporter on the Visiter in 1969-70 and have many mixed memories of events around that time.

There was huge controversy when the bandstand was replaced by a hideous fountain known as The Cascade. Meant to be a focal point for Lord Street, vandals soon put detergent in its bubbling waters, sending blobs of foam everywhere.

One day, I was having lunch in a Lord Street cafe when I heard a familiar voice. Film star Trevor Howard, of Brief Encounter fame, was having a fry-up at the next table. I also reported on the ghostly goings-on at the huge Birkdale Palace Hotel, which was being demolished.

Now, The Cascade is gone and the visitors once more enjoy music from the bandstand.

Duke Street reminds us of Southport's founder.

PALACE HOTEL
BIRKDALE

LORD ST
STATION

OPERA
HOUSE

SEASIDE ELEGANCE

1910: Southport's Lord Street, including landmarks such as the Cheshire Lines station, Opera House and Winter Gardens

WINTER
GARDENS

ROYAL
HOTEL

"STRIKES ME WE'VE LANDED IN CHINA....!"

GOING 'ABROAD'

Left, comic postcard featuring the 'place with the longest name'. Right, me, aged 11, in an old car. Below, a roadside halt in North Wales in 1962

Off to the Hills

GENERATIONS of holidaymakers have headed to North Wales for day trips and holidays at varying speeds and levels of comfort.

A century ago, such a journey was fraught with difficulties, with few garages and back-up on the open road.

Liverpool boasted top motor showrooms displaying expensive cars only available to the affluent.

Watson's in Renshaw Street were agents for Rolls-Royce, Sunbeam and Vauxhall, while Blake's in Rodney Street catered for Wolseley, Ford and Buick.

Some people had chauffeurs but increasing numbers were getting behind the wheel themselves. In those days, before the Mersey Tunnel, cars were taken across the Mersey on luggage boats. Cars and motorbikes were charged tolls of 3d (1p) per wheel at Queensferry.

Resorts and tourist spots had a choice of good hotels. Three of the best at Caernarfon were the Royal and Prince of Wales in Bangor Street and the Royal Sportsman in Castle Street.

Once ensconced, the early motorist could explore the stunning countryside of Snowdonia and Anglesey.

A 1926 postcard lampoons the reaction of two English motorists seeing a sign for Llanfairpwllgwyngyll on the road to Holyhead.

My childhood memories of visiting North Wales in the 1950s and 1960s often feature the difficulties getting there. We would take the Crosville coach from a bustling depot in Edge Lane and all would be serene until we reached Queensferry.

Today, dual carriageways take the traveller smoothly and swiftly on their way, but it was once a very different story. I remember one particular horror journey in the 1950s when a monumental traffic jam greeted us. Vehicles stopped and nothing moved. A family in one car got out and had a picnic by the roadside before things started going again.

We spent two holidays in an idyllic cottage called Pen-y-Ffridd halfway up a mountain at Nebo, near Penygroes. An abandoned car graced the adjacent farmyard. I was pictured admiring the view through the sunroof in July 1959.

The jalopy had a Liverpool LV registration and an opening in the radiator for the starting handle.

We stopped at the cottage again in 1962, once more travelling by coach. The owner helpfully left a handcart by the bus stop so we could wheel our luggage a mile or so to our destination.

My aunt visited in her A40 and is pictured, above, with my parents on a visit to a local pottery.

Two years later, we had our first motoring holiday, in my brother's car, to Llangollen. Being an adventurous 15-year-old, my parents gave me £1 and I travelled from Liverpool on three buses to check out the cottage before we booked it.

Elemental Force

THE ferocious storm brought claps of thunder that seemed to herald the end of the world with violent crashes echoing around the Wirral countryside.

Some people cowered in their homes, praying that the horrible cacophony would end and bring some peace.

It was a stormy June 14, 1890, and, as the Cheshire Observer colourfully reported: "A ball of fire fell from one of the clouds and struck the hill opposite Mr Woodward's shop in Hoylake Road.

"It first dug a trench a foot deep and a yard long and, entering the ground, tunnelled through the earth and matted roots and heather for a space of five yards until it emerged again through some red sandstone on the hillside.

"The rock was burst asunder as if by a charge of dynamite and pieces of it a foot broad were scattered for a number of yards around."

It was as if Thor, the god of thunder, had emerged bellowing from his stone set on Thurstaston Common – a place of wonderment for countless generations.

A later storm is seen in our postcard picture. On the seafront, waves smashed against the promenade alongside New Brighton Pier in its Edwardian heyday. A group of people huddle out of the wind, drawn by a strange fascination to watch the crashing breakers.

STORMY TIMES

Left, a ferocious storm hits New Brighton. Below, Heswall Stores in 1904, emblazoned with adverts for Fry's chocolate and cocoa

Liverpool Bay has always been a place of danger when nature unleashes its fury with gale-force winds and mountainous seas.

This has not deterred people commuting from Liverpool – even in the days when the only way to cross the Mersey was by boat.

A storm of a different kind was reported by the Cheshire Observer on February 25, 1888: "Great indignation was expressed in Heswall after the third escape from Upton Asylum of Charles Jones, a Heswall mason, who is stated to be a dangerous lunatic.

"Jones has left each time with the avowed intention of murdering his wife, who lives in Heswall, and after his last escape was caught upon the common near his wife's residence."

Despite a big police search, he was still at large wearing his asylum clothes. Happier news came in November 1893, when a new mail van was delivered which was "more in keeping with this rising locality".

Painted in scarlet and yellow, it was emblazoned with the Royal Arms. At this time, Heswall Post Office was run by Mrs Jane Smallwood whose late husband William was postmaster for many years. In Victorian times, Heswall, like other districts, grew from a small rural community into a dormitory village for those seeking an escape from their urban surroundings.

Comedy
of Errors

THE family of entertainers arrived at Lime Street Station with their luggage including props for their act at a nearby theatre.

Comic duettists Mr and Mrs Leno and their clog-dancing sons had been engaged to appear at the Adelphi Theatre in Liverpool's Christian Street. One of the sons, Dan, hailed a porter who loaded his handcart with the Leno luggage – an odd assortment including a trick bedstead.

The porter was told to take it all to the Adelphi. He touched his cap and trundled out of the station.

Dan Leno (1860-1904) had been an entertainer since the age of four and later became arguably the greatest ever British stand-up comedian.

DAN LENO

One of the finest comics
Britain ever produced

ADELPHI

The long-gone theatre's name was shared with the hotel. Below, the first incarnation of Liverpool's famous hotel, to which the porter mistakenly took the Lenos' luggage

After seeing off the porter, Dan went for a walk around the town. He bought a couple of cakes then sauntered over to the theatre to find no sign of the porter, cart or luggage.

Dan went back to the station and searched along Lime Street until raised voices stopped him in his tracks.

The porter, struggling with the trick bedstead on his back, stood on the steps of the Adelphi Hotel demanding admission. Two liveried servants at the high-class establishment refused point-blank to let him in.

Dan was horrified to see the rest of the luggage strewn over the muddy street after being chucked out of the hotel. He recalled: "My porter was undaunted. He had been told to put the things in the Adelphi and he would have them in if it killed him."

Two cheeky boys had found a stuffed dog to use as a football. Dan picked it up and went over to the porter to explain things.

"I shall never forget the look on that man's face if I live to be 99. I never saw a man look with such earnest desire to take a human life as he did. Had he raised the bedstead and brained me where I stood I should not have been at all surprised. I should have been sorry but not surprised."

By this time a crowd had gathered – they booed as Dan and the porter loaded the property back on to the cart. The bystanders then followed the cart in a procession towards the Adelphi Theatre.

They had no sooner turned into Christian Street when one of the cart's wheels fell off, pitching its load again into the street.

"For the 14th time our porter repeated his entire vocabulary of obscene and profane terms of general abuse and condemnation."

Dan gave him all his remaining cash – a shilling (5p). The porter took the money, staggered, snorted, clenched his fists and stormed off.

Death-defying Tightrope Feat

A GALE was blowing, but the tightrope walker insisted on performing his death-defying feats, ignoring pleas to come down.

Charles Blondin approached the centre of the rope clutching a long balancing pole while bracing himself against the wind.

The crowd gasped as the daredevil prepared to stand on his head 75ft above the ground without any safety equipment.

The boss of Eastham Gardens, fearing a tragedy, yelled at him to abandon his performance.

Sixty-year-old Blondin paused and seemed to have second thoughts.

"He had to content himself by lying flat on the rope thus escaping the gusts that swept around him," reported the Cheshire Observer.

Blondin stood up and carried on to the other end of the rope: "To the amazement of the assemblage he proceeded to bandage his eyes but so strong was the gale that twice the handkerchief was nearly blown from his hands. "

Just to make it more challenging, he put a sack over his head before walking back along the rope without mishap. There was thunderous applause as he descended to his tent, blue with cold.

It was Easter 1884, and Frenchman Blondin (1824-1897) was starting a three-month season at the gardens, served by a ferry from Liverpool and a popular resort for generations.

Blondin had been an international star for 50 years since starting his acrobatic career as The Boy Wonder.

His feats at Eastham, remarkable in themselves, almost paled into insignificance when compared to his incredible exploits at Niagara Falls more than 20 years earlier.

Blondin walked over the roaring waterfall on a three-inch hemp rope stretching 1,100 feet more than 160ft above the raging torrents, watched by thousands.

His numerous Niagara escapades included crossing blindfolded, in a sack, trundling a wheelbarrow, on stilts, carrying his manager on his back, sitting down midway while he cooked and ate an omelette and standing on a chair with only one chair leg on the rope.

Blondin was paid huge fees for his performances and carried on tightrope walking into his 70s. He settled in England and died peacefully at home, aged 73.

The Eastham Ferry operated from the Middle Ages (run by monks from St Werburgh's Abbey) until 1929.

A pier was built in the late 1700s to serve passengers and goods. The opening of railway links heralded a decline which was reversed when the Eastham Ferry Hotel was built in 1846. A decorative arch was constructed at the entrance to the pleasure gardens in 1897 to commemorate Queen Victoria's Diamond Jubilee.

Eastham Country Park remains a popular place to visit with its fine woodland walks and river views.

RIVER TRAVEL

Wirral ferries at Liverpool's Pier Head in 1904

DAREDEVIL
Charles Blondin arrives in England with one of his tightropes

SHOPPING & FASHION

From the Bond Street of the north, to a city centre menagerie of wild and exotic beasts

38360. JY.

BOLD STREET.
LIVERPOOL.

Bold & Brass

An 1885 engraving showing boys' fashions

JUST SEW
Above, Paris fashions, including riding clothes from 1851

IT WAS Liverpool's top shopping area for more than a century – but it actually started off as a field where ropes were made for sailing ships.

Bold Street was originally residential, when merchants lived on their business premises, where they could keep an eye on things.

Gradually, wealthy people moved out to the suburbs, where they could have large gardens surrounding their beautiful homes. One of the last to live in Bold Street was Thomas Tobin, who moved out in 1838.

The area was then almost totally given over to shops selling the finest goods money could buy – in particular, the latest fashions.

Bold Street was justifiably compared to London's Bond Street because of the excellence of the goods on offer to those with the cash.

Madame Jane Clarke was one of the popular dressmakers in mid-Victorian times and two other stores that attracted fashion-conscious ladies in the 1870s were Bright's and Woolright's.

Carriages would clatter into Bold Street from the outskirts of Liverpool. The tinted postcard from about 1905 on the previous page shows a lady in her conveyance giving instructions to the coachman outside J Faraday and Sons.

Another fine coach drawn by two white horses pulls up behind. Over the road is the Lyceum club, which housed a fine library, and in the distance is St Luke's Church, now a ruin after being bombed in the Blitz.

My grandmother May Kendrick attended St Luke's and our family Bible was awarded to her as the school scripture prize at Christmas 1879 when she was aged 11. It was later used to record the births of her nine children, starting with the oldest, William, in 1893 to the youngest, George – my father – in 1911.

Bold Street may have been a glamorous place, but it was surrounded by businesses and factories. My great-grandfather managed a mill in nearby Wood Street.

Children had their own fashions and two happy boys are seen in 1885 – one wears a sailor suit, a particular favourite among better-off children in Liverpool. Large billowing skirts known as crinolines were in vogue for a long time and the Paris fashions of 1851 would have been copied by dressmakers in Bold Street.

One model wears riding clothes including a top hat – she would have ridden side-saddle on hunts in Lancashire and Cheshire.

Shopping trends change and one of the last traditional dressmakers, Cripps, shut down in the early 1970s – at about the time the Lyceum also closed.

However, Bold Street remains a vibrant and exciting shopping area.

Sunday Best

FAMILIES would head for the Pier Head or one of the city's parks to make the most of Sunday – and all would be in their best clothes.

This was the one day of the week the majority of people had off work and they made the most of it.

A hundred years ago, people made their own outfits or bought them from the many specialist outfitters.

Tafner's in Elliot Street and Dale Street claimed to be Liverpool's leading outfitter. Here were all the latest ties and everything new in men's headwear, while ladies' and gents' gloves were another speciality.

My father went to a studio to have his picture taken, aged five, in his new suit, complete with Eton collar and flat cap.

It was 1916 and George was about to start school at Heyworth Street in Everton. The youngest of nine children, when Grandma took him the teacher exclaimed: "Not another one, Mrs Guy!"

Dad would have been just one of the myriad children dressed up for their weekly outings.

As far as I know, he never had a sailor suit, but quite a few of the better-off children in Liverpool would have been decked out like the three boys proudly saluting in an advert for Allenbury's Foods.

The company produced malted milk products sold throughout Britain and the Empire.

Sailor suits were popular with generations of children up to the Second World War. Queen Victoria popularised the fashion by dressing up her sons – and sometimes her daughters – in the suits.

By the 1870s, sailor suits were among the most popular styles. They would have been a common sight among the crowds enjoying visits to New Brighton and Southport.

A ride up to the top of New Brighton Tower was one of the highlights, while the less adventurous could enjoy the sands and the funfair.

Victorian children wore broad-brimmed straw sailor hats. By Edwardian times, they had switched to the flat-topped caps.

There was plenty to do on the Sunday outings and another popular destination was Eastham with its pleasure grounds in the woods next to the ferry.

The day started with visits to church and Sunday School, which also organised outings. For the more adventurous, Helsby was a popular venue with its trek up to the top of the crag.

Trippers were rewarded with breathtaking views across to Liverpool and the Welsh hills.

Virtually everyone went by public transport and those with less cash simply walked.

When he got older, father would hike for miles in the countryside around Liverpool.

On one memorable occasion, he walked with the family dog Tom from Everton to Knowsley and back.

Walk This Way

IT was 1916, at the height of the First World War, and cinemas were packed with people determined to forget their troubles by watching silent films which were often accompanied by live music.

Charlie Chaplin was a huge comedy star and one of his hit films was The Floorwalker, which poked fun at the authority figures who were common sights in Liverpool and other major shopping areas. They were often tall, former military men whose job was to assist customers like the ubiquitous Captain Peacock in TV comedy Are You Being Served? set in an old-fashioned department store.

His catchphrase "Are you free?" and the response from counter staff "I'm free!" have entered the national psyche.

Even then floorwalkers were an anachronism – today, the nearest equivalent is a floor manager. However, in Edwardian times they were an essential part of the shopping experience and knew how to deal with awkward customers.

The emphasis was on service – the better stores aimed to pamper their customers. At the top end of the scale in Bold Street, clients were often treated like royalty, offered comfy chairs and refreshments.

This was long before the concept of self-service, now virtually the norm, swept through the High Street after World War II.

Bunney's store in Church Street is seen in 1910, its windows stacked high with enticing goods. No doubt the floorwalkers were kept busy throughout the day in this popular emporium.

Those entering Frisby Dyke's in Lord Street looking uncertain would be pounced upon by the floorwalker. Flowers or feathers? Ribbons or bows? He would be there to direct customers and help supervise sales.

Lewis's, at the end of Lime Street, was another domain of the floorwalker, who needed a thorough knowledge of the latest stock and what was, or was not, available.

A coloured postcard drawn by W Milne Black in 1903 shows a very smartly-dressed floorwalker decked out in cravat, frock coat and spats. It is captioned The Walking Contest "Step this way, walk this way."

AH writes imaginatively to Miss Price in Belfast: "He is just a shop-walker and a champion at that for he leads every time. How would you like to walk him?"

My mum worked in Blackler's in the 1930s and had many shopfloor stories. In the early evening, men came dressed in dinner suits to purchase black ties. Mother was among assistants sometimes summoned by the floorwalker to fasten one while the customer stood with his chin up.

Years later, I asked her how to tie one but she'd forgotten. So I taught myself by tying one around my knee.

RETAIL THERAPY

Bunney's on Church Street, Liverpool. Opposite page, a postcard dating from 1903, showing a smartly-dressed store floorwalker

Snapshots of Life

S HE was a popular figure in the community for many years and in her spare time enjoyed photography as a hobby.

In late Victorian and Edwardian times, Marion Fergie (1869-1961) recorded people in West Derby, Liverpool.

At this time, there were about 60 large villas and mansions around the prosperous village dominated by St Mary's Church and Croxteth Hall, ancestral homes of the Earls of Sefton.

Miss Fergie, as she was universally known, liked to photograph people in their Sunday best after they had been to church.

She worked as a postmistress and assistant chemist but also had an unofficial role as a wise confidante to those in need of advice. People would go to her shop and sit down – this was a signal that they wanted to talk once the coast was clear.

The West Derby Society's collection of 156 original glass plates gives a strongly female slant on life in northern England more than a century ago.

Marion focuses mainly on fashions, children and characters, including men in uniforms. It is believed she developed and printed her own photographs as she had access to a dark room at the chemist's.

Several pictures feature The Barracks, a group of tenements that stood behind the West Derby Courthouse until the 1930s. A tram driver poses with his family before going to work – West Derby was served by trams from the 1880s to 1949.

A boy in knickerbockers is captured with his family in a garden setting. A military man proudly wears his medals. A languid lady takes her ease among the trees.

Others show cosy parlours or draughty churches including some in Cartmel, Lake District.

There are lots of charming studies of children in their best clothes – the boys in Eton collars and girls in lace-up boots. Ladies stand straight in floor-length skirts and men sport frock coats and top hats. Animals including dogs and rabbits are also featured.

People may live in very humble homes but they often dress up to the nines – for church, social occasions and to work in the big smart houses of West Derby as grooms, maids and nannies.

FAMILY PORTRAITS

These photos of families by photographer Marion Fergie give us a glimpse into life in West Derby

Mother pauses from the household chores to pose with her smartly-dressed sons, demure young women stand in neat gardens, a handsome boy leans nonchalantly against a wall while neighbours come together for a group photograph. A wedding group shows the sharp contrast between the fine clothes and the relatively ordinary surroundings – the bride is probably a young widow as she does not wear a bridal gown.

We know virtually nothing about the people or their pets in the photographs.

OLD CITY CHAPTERS

Books old and new in Howell's, at 83, Church Street, above, and, left, the hat and cap showroom at Mander & Allender's on Dale Street

Fancy a camel – or elephant – from Cross the Wild Beast Merchant in St Paul's Square?

In-store Safari

THE city centre menagerie boasted roaring lions, trumpeting elephants and countless exotic birds.

Cross the Wild Beast Merchant – slogan: "Known throughout the civilised and uncivilised world" – was the strangest store in Liverpool.

Situated in St Paul's Square, off Old Hall Street, it was one of many contrasting emporia to tempt every kind of shopper.

Cross pledged to supply anything from tiny humming birds to great beasts. There were hordes of foreign birds, lions and tigers, monkeys, snakes ("by the mile"), camels, elephants, bears, zebras and wolves.

It was 1906 and in those less enlightened times Liverpool was ideally placed to import animals from across the globe.

Potential buyers and the general public could view the hundreds of creatures that arrived every week.

Cross supplied aviaries and zoos in the city's parks as well as other towns and cities – and also the Government.

Liverpool merchants liked to have peacocks strutting around the grounds of their mansions while many humbler homes had parrots and monkeys.

As well as department stores such as Lewis's, there were many specialist retailers to supply more mundane needs.

Tafner's in Elliot Street and Dale Street offered all sorts of clothes and accessories. My mum was a young assistant there some years later and told many anecdotes about the staff and customers.

Edward Howell, at 83, Church Street, was a mecca for the Edwardian book-lover, stocking an amazing 300,000 volumes, ancient and modern. It claimed to be "one of the largest in the Empire".

Over in Dale Street, Mander & Allender was founded in the reign of George IV (1826). An advert showed

the hat and cap showroom groaning with shelves of headwear at a time when everyone wore a hat.

Archer & Sons, on St George's Crescent (top of Lord Street), stocked "talking machines" (gramophones).

The ornate contraptions played records amplified by horns. An advert asked: "If you are thinking of going in for a Talking Machine, why not get the best? You can get a Genuine Gramophone from 30 shillings." (£1.50)

For those with lots of spare cash, John Byrne & Son, of 10, Bold Street, stocked diamonds, fine jewels, watches, clocks and antiques.

Edwardian keep-fit enthusiasts were catered for by the Howe Electrical Engineering Co, in Redcross Street.

One perhaps dubious product was the patented Howe Electrical Attachment that could be wired up to chest expanders.

This promised "exercise and pleasure combined" – greater strength for athletes, more nerve power for motorists and sportsmen and better health for invalids.

It came in a range of sizes for children, men and women and was "highly recommended by the medical profession".

ON THE MOVE

Pioneering railways, a pit stop at Compton's and an angry mob out for revenge...

The Age of the Train

Nell Guy and her elder son, David, snapped by a wartime street photographer. Above, Central Station

LIVERPOOL pioneered modern railways with the opening of services to Manchester, and soon Britain – and later the world – followed.

As the city grew, more lines were needed to provide links not only to other towns and cities but local and surrounding areas.

Once the railway arrived, the developers followed. From 1830, people realised that they did not need to live close to their work.

New houses appeared around the recently-opened stations. Many were for better-off people who could afford regular commuting. From Kirkby to Hoylake and Southport to Gateacre, increasing numbers of villas sprang up.

The age of mass travel had arrived and continues today with controversial plans to build major new lines.

Victorian railway builders were given almost a blank cheque to carve up the countryside. Even the landed gentry and aristocracy seemed powerless to stop the remorseless rise of the train.

There were few planning laws to hold things up – once land was acquired, work began.

People would arrive at a churchyard to find the grave of a loved one had disappeared under a new railway. Beautiful valleys and dales were criss-crossed by viaducts and bridges.

Liverpool's Central Station opened in 1874, built by the Cheshire Lines as an alternative route to Manchester. Originally, it offered only above ground services – the underground beneath the Mersey to Wirral opened in 1892.

Central Station is pictured on the previous page in a 1904

photograph. No motors are visible. Two electric trams head towards the Pier Head surrounded by horse-drawn vehicles, including Hansom cabs and goods wagons.

A handcart is flanked by three men carrying sandwich boards advertising shops and attractions.

We often travelled from Central Station underground on outings to the Wirral. Mum was leaving the station about 1944 with my brother, David, when they were snapped by a street photographer, see picture, above.

They would take photographs of likely customers (usually families), hand out a card and the pictures could be collected later.

Bidston Hill was a favourite place reached by train and bus. We would walk through

the bracken to the rocks by the windmill and sit admiring the view while sharing a chocolate bar.

The three-storey Central Station high-level building fronted a 65ft-high arched shed where trains arrived and departed.

There were six platforms, with trains serving Manchester, London, Hull, Harwich, Stockport and Southport.

It was closed under the notorious Beeching Axe – most services were switched to other stations in 1966. The last service, to stations in south Liverpool, ran until 1972.

The original Central Station was demolished in 1973, although the underground station remains as a key element of the transport network.

Grimestoppers

The driver's cab in the newly-electrified Mersey Railway

PEOPLE flocked to experience the new form of travel which took them into a new dimension under the waves.

The Mersey Railway linked Liverpool to Birkenhead and had been a dream for decades. Planners realised that a rapid form of transport under the River Mersey would boost the growth of the region.

It would free travellers from the vagaries of weather and tides which could considerably delay ferry boats and other river traffic.

However, the railway, opened to the public in 1886, was a victim of its own success, caused by the steam trains used on the service. Choking fumes filled the tunnels and soon everything from stations to carriages were covered with sooty grime. A heavy, polluted atmosphere pervaded, making the journey something of a claustrophobic ordeal. Commuters would cover their faces with handkerchiefs and scarves to keep out the smoke. Clothes were smudged with soot.

Passenger figures declined, although 10m people still travelled every year when permission was given to electrify the railway. Contractors had to carry out the conversion without interrupting services, a task requiring meticulous planning.

The last steam train chugged through the tunnels at midnight on May 3, 1903, before electricity took over. Travellers were delighted with the new carriages and the clean atmosphere that electricity allowed.

The electric Overhead Railway alongside Liverpool's docks had opened in 1893, but the power system was still a relative novelty. Many houses were still lit by gas and it was some years before electricity became widely available.

Power for the Mersey Railway was provided by a generating station next to Hamilton Square Station.

In 1866, an Act of Parliament had been passed for the construction of a pneumatic railway using compressed air or a vacuum, but the plan was eventually dropped in favour of steam. Before the main tunnel was built, engineers dug an experimental passage through the red sandstone to test the suitability of the rock. The trial tunnel was later used to ventilate the railway.

The main tunnel had an extreme width of 26ft and a height of 19ft from the rails to the top of the arch. The first electric trains consisted of two or three carriages between motor cars at either end. There were 48 seats in first class and 64 in second.

Each motor car was mounted on two four-wheel bogies. Air brakes supplemented with hand brakes were fitted. The tracks, in 30ft sections, were supported by between 13 and 16 sleepers per length.

Travelling on the Mersey Railway for the first time remains a thrilling experience, with generations of children telling their parents: "I haven't seen any fish yet."

A first-class electric carriage on the electrified Liverpool to Birkenhead railway

Motor Magic

PIONEERING motorists visiting Liverpool were given detailed information on routes to and from the city to avoid pit stops due to bad roads and other obstacles. This was the era when automobilists – as they were also known – were a minority and the butt of music hall jokes and cartoons.

A popular song was He Had To Get Under, Get Out and Get Under, which stressed the number of times a car might break down.

A comic postcard shows three men, including a uniformed chauffeur, pulling a very smart motor with the caption: 'We had a mishap but all pulled through.'

Until Henry Ford introduced relatively cheap cars through mass production, motoring was the preserve of the well-off. The first car journeys were fraught with inconvenience because there were no garages and petrol had to be bought from hardware stores.

Motorists needed to be competent

mechanics because there were no breakdown services. Drivers and their passengers wore goggles and voluminous clothing to protect them from rain, mud and dust.

By 1914, things were getting easier for motorists, but journeys were still hazardous and unpredictable.

The Michelin Guide for 1914 is full of fascinating information designed to smooth the way for drivers.

Four routes in and out of Liverpool are identified at a time when signposts still towered

WE HAD A MISHAP BUT ALL PULLED THROUGH

TRAVELLER'S REST

The Compton's Hotel in Church Street, main picture, was the destination of choice – if the car made it

the height of horse-drawn mail coaches, making them difficult to read from a car. The routes are via Dale Street/Vauxhall Road, Byrom Street/Scotland Road, London Road/ Kensington and Lime Street/ Leece Street. Directions are also provided to the Pier Head.

Travellers are given two routes to Southport, for example. It was a bad road if they went through Formby (before the bypass) but the road was good by way of Ormskirk – and the distance about the same.

Detailed information is provided for hotels. Compton's in Church Street, Liverpool, (pictured) provided a free garage for 20 cars. Breakfast and lunch each cost 2s 6d (12.5p) while dinner would set you back 3s 6d (17.5p).

Garages and motor suppliers included W Watson & Co in Renshaw St (agents for Rolls-Royce, Sunbeam and Vauxhall) and Kerslake's in West Derby Village (telephone Old Swan 589).

Once you got to Southport, among

the many hotels on offer was the huge Birkdale Palace, where your chauffeur could be accommodated for six shillings (30p) a night.

Among detailed excursions is a 122-mile round trip from Chester to Llandudno through Betws-y-Coed and Rhuddlan. The bridge toll at Queensferry is 3d (just over 1p) a wheel.

The guide is also peppered with adverts promoting everything from car horns and mudguards to pyjamas and typewriters.

Act of Revenge

THE Liverpool pork butcher was well established in the community, but the sinking of the luxury liner Lusitania during the First World War turned his customers into a baying mob who destroyed his business.

In scenes mirrored in other British towns and cities, shops and offices run by people of German origin were attacked.

The sinking of the 31,550-ton Lusitania by the U-20 submarine on May 7, 1915, sent out a wave of revulsion – nowhere was it felt more deeply than Liverpool. The Cunarder had been plying back and forth to New York since she was built in 1907. Many Liverpool people served on the city's favourite ship.

Christian Yaag came out of his shop at 7 Great George Street smoking his pipe, wondering why so many people were outside. Although born in Germany, with two nephews serving in the British army, he was not immune from the people's wrath.

They wanted revenge on all Germans and Yaag was beaten to the ground. A volley of stones and bricks smashed his windows and the mob trashed the shop. The wrecked premises is pictured later after police had arrived to restore order.

The Lusitania sank in just 18 minutes after being torpedoed off the Old Head of Kinsale in Ireland – nearly 1,200 people died. There were chaotic scenes as people scrambled for the lifeboats. Minutes before they had been enjoying lunch and the leisure facilities on the Cunard line's floating palace that had built up a great reputation for service and comfort.

Unlike the Titanic three years earlier, the 787ft-long Lusitania sank in relatively shallow water (about 300ft deep) and her bows were resting on the seabed as her stern sank from view. For a time, just her four huge funnels were visible before they disappeared beneath the waves.

One of the lifeboats narrowly missed a funnel as survivors frantically rowed clear of the foundering vessel. Some survivors managed to swim to the coast and local fishermen sailed out to pick up others.

Captain William Turner, who lived in Crosby, stayed until the end and miraculously survived after floating off the wreck. He is pictured in Queenstown after the disaster. There were many Americans on board and among the 123 who died were wealthy society figures, writers and artists.

There are many exhibits from Lusitania in the Merseyside Maritime Museum, including a deckchair, a cushion from the First Class smoking room and lifebuoy. When war came again with Germany in 1939, the British authorities did not want repetitions of scenes such as the wrecking of Yaag's. German and other enemy nationals were interned until they were given clearance.

Captain Turner. Opposite page, the sinking of Lusitania provoked revenge attacks against those in Liverpool who had German links

R.M.S. LUSITANIA.

CHARLES J. DE LACY

HISTORIC

A contemporary image of Lime Street.
Below, the station frontage in 1826

Lime Street Story

THOUSANDS of passengers using Lime Street Station during the Easter holidays pass over the site of Waterworth's Fields, where Liverpudlians once enjoyed themselves on the edge of the town.

The first station, designed by leading architect John Foster, was built in 1836 as an imposing terminus for the Liverpool to Manchester Railway.

Lime Street was originally a rural byway at the top of a bracken-covered slope leading down to the Liver Pool which gave the town its name.

Lime kilns and windmills dotted the landscape swept then, as now, by the prevailing westerly winds bringing the tang of the open sea inland.

This was a bracing spot and a path led to the Fall Well, which supplied residents with pure, life enhancing spring water.

Liverpool was growing in prosperity and tentacles of development were creeping towards Lime Street as every year passed.

Waterworth's Fields were popular with young people taking part in sports and local customs.

Every Shrove Tuesday, as the rigours of Lent approached, boys enjoyed a boisterous and cruel game. Watched and cheered by family and friends, groups of lads stood in line with their arms tied behind their backs.

A cockerel was let loose on to the grass to be chased by the boys. The terrified bird would twist, turn and flutter as it was pursued by the mob of pinioned youngsters. According to the rules of this ancient sport, they could capture the cockerel by either flinging themselves on to it or grabbing it with their teeth – no easy task. Whoever caught the bird kept it – quite a prize when poultry was kept for eggs and food.

These high jinks ended when the first station was built. A coloured engraving shows the grand entrance of the new terminus in the year it opened.

Four large gateways give access to the railway – horse-drawn carriages come and go while elegant ladies and gentlemen saunter in the sunlight.

There is no sense of the hustle and bustle that was later the hallmark of the trains as they steamed from place to place.

The arrival of the railway led to the development of Lime Street. Liverpool's civic leaders wanted a magnificent building to greet travellers – and St George's Hall was conceived.

A drawing by Herdman shows Lime Street more than two decades later in 1857 – the two ornamental granite columns were known as The Candlesticks. They were later moved to Sefton Park and the stone lions shifted to their present positions facing the station.

I was told as a child that the huge beasts stuck their tongues out at the stroke of midnight.

War of the Wagons

LIVERPOOL'S dock road reverberated with the clopping of horses' hooves and the rumbling of iron-rimmed cart wheels as cargoes were shifted back and forth.

The horse still dominated the roads in late Victorian times. Heavily-laden wagons lumbered between ship and warehouse. Buses, hackney cabs and private carriages carried people on short journeys. It was 1898 and change was in the air. Novelists like HG Wells were enthralling readers with tales of space travel – this was the year he wrote War of the Worlds.

Merseyside's commercial elite realised that new types of transport would take over from horses.

They needed to find the best, most

BIG DAY

Above, the LIFU steam lorry loaded with wooden barrels. Right, judges and competitors gather outside the Swan at Aughton. Below, John Brodie

efficient vehicles for the job.

Petrol-driven cars were appearing on the roads, but they were the preserve of the rich. At this time, they were not seen as a viable alternative for mass road transport.

Early drivers had to be self-sufficient or employ a chauffeur. There were no roadside garages or back-up services – you filled up with fuel at the local ironmonger's.

Steam-powered vehicles were seen as the future for commercial road transport. They were reliable and robust – huge steamrollers were employed to flatten newly-laid road surfaces. The Self-Propelled Traffic Association held a five-day competition to boost the most efficient ways to get goods to and from inland towns as well as dockside warehouses.

It was also a fun event, rather like the London to Brighton run immortalised in the film Genevieve.

Various bigwigs were involved in the Liverpool branch of the Association, including top ship-owner Alfred Holt. The city's visionary engineer John Brodie was among the judges. The chief object of the trials was to find a suitable self-propelled wagon which could economically replace horse haulage and compete with railway rates over considerable distances.

Competitors were issued with route maps to make identical journeys between Liverpool and outlying districts. Each trial run was between 30 and 40 miles. Although 10 vehicles were originally entered for the competition, only four steam lorries took part. Two were built by Thornycroft, one by Leyland and the fourth was entered by the Liquid Fuel Engineering Company (LIFU) of the Isle of Wight.

Excitement built up and then, on May 23, competitors gathered at the Princes Dock ready for the off.

Precise rules were laid down and two contrasting routes followed on different days, accompanied by the judges in a motor carriage followed by back-up and other interested parties. One route included a depot at the Swan Inn in Aughton before proceeding through Rainford and back to Liverpool via Knotty Ash.

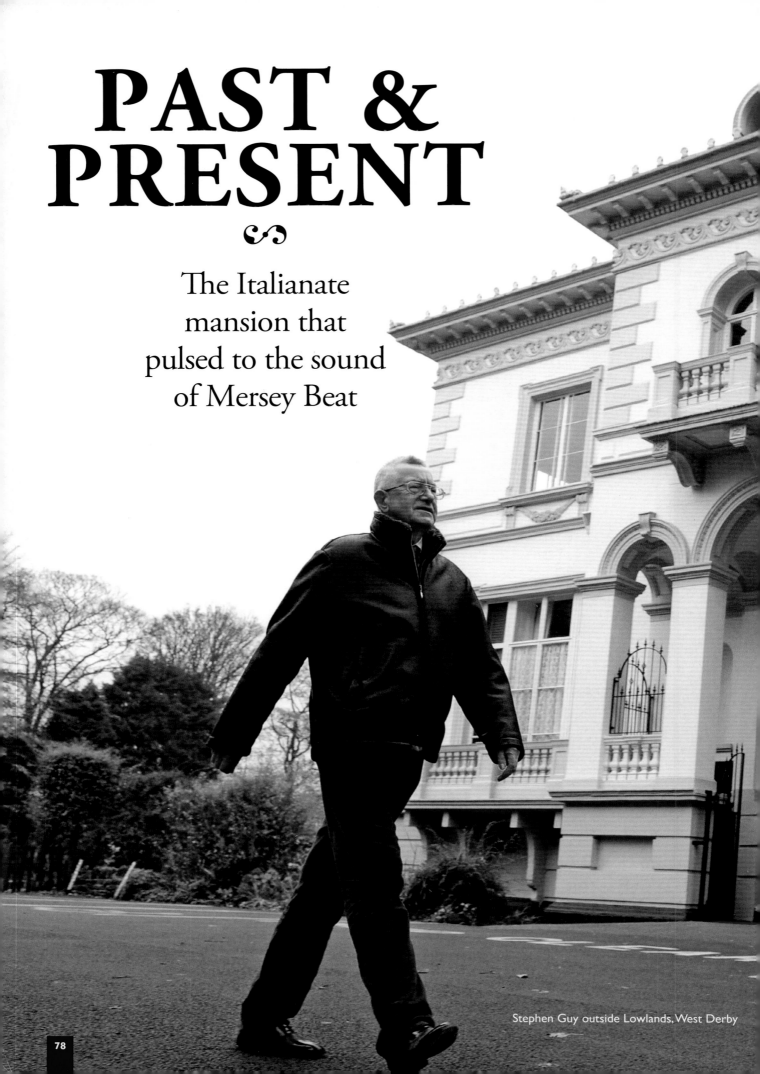

PAST & PRESENT

The Italianate mansion that pulsed to the sound of Mersey Beat

Stephen Guy outside Lowlands, West Derby

Heart of the Community

THE successful architect decided to design and build a new home for his growing family away from the hazards of the town.

Thomas Haigh lived on Gambier Terrace not far from his busy office in Liverpool's fashionable Bold Street. It was 1844 and Liverpool was booming with ever-expanding docks and seemingly inexhaustible business opportunities, and 39-year-old Thomas was making a lot of money.

He and his wife, Jane, set about finding a site for their new home, choosing Haymans Green in West Derby Village.

It was a very different environment from nearby smoky, cramped Liverpool where life-expectancy was just 19, because so many children died from disease and bad conditions.

The Haighs wanted healthier surroundings for their five children.

Thomas bought two building plots so they had an impressive garden for their 38-room Italianate mansion.

This brought the benefits of light and air while impressing potential clients as well as family and friends.

The Haighs took up residence in 1846 and four more children quickly followed. Several other families lived there before the death of last resident Margaret Withers in 1930.

She brought up eight children after the death of her stockbroker husband in 1899.

Lowlands was bought by neighbour Alderman Ernest Cookson and used by the Inland Revenue during and after the Second World War.

In 1957, Alderman Cookson sold Lowlands to its current owners, the West Derby Community Association.

Lowlands had been wrecked but an enthusiastic team of volunteers and professionals restored the building.

Around 1959, teenagers started a basement youth club which flourished and started to attract young musicians.

Dubbed the Pillar Club, it was attended by The Beatles, Searchers, Gerry and the Pacemakers, Billy J Kramer, Hollies and Hermanís Hermits to name just a few.

Fifteen-year-old George Harrison played with the resident band, the Les Stewart Quartet.

Legend has it that at this time, George's other group, the Quarrymen, failed a Lowlands audition.

Ironically, as The Beatles, they later enjoyed huge popularity at the neighbouring Casbah Coffee Club.

One day in 1962, Brian Epstein, who managed the Beatles and other fledgling stars, arrived at the Pillar Club to see one of his acts. He flew into a rage at being asked to pay admission, storming off vowing never to let any of his musicians appear there again, a pledge he kept.

I have been a Lowlands director since 2002 and helped secure a £1.1m grant from the Heritage Lottery Fund to refurbish and restore the Grade II-listed building.

It reopened to the public in 2009 and continues as the West Derby Community Centre, a registered charity. Around 20 groups and organisations meet at Lowlands, which is also ideal for a variety of functions, including anniversaries, christenings and funerals.

Details at www.lowlands.org.uk or telephone 0151 226 5352.

HERITAGE SITE

The staircase viewed from above and below, the main hall, originally three rooms, with Rococo Revival ceilings from 1846. Bottom, the Over 21s club opened in November 1962, used by older members of the Lowlands Youth Club in the 1960s

GREAT MAGAZINES FROM THE HEART OF THE CITY

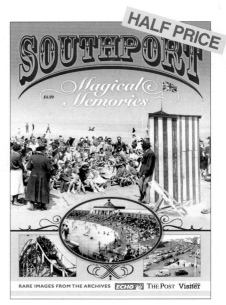

HALF PRICE

NOW £2.50
SOUTHPORT MAGICAL MEMORIES

A rollercoaster ride through a packed photo album of the much-loved seaside resort

HALF PRICE

NOW £2.50
RIVER CITY: PAST, PRESENT & FUTURE

The people, the landscape, the docks, and all those ships that played their parts in history

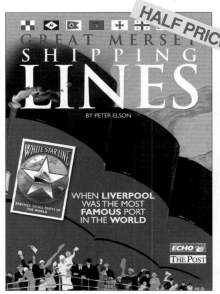

HALF PRICE

NOW £2.50
GREAT MERSEY SHIPPING LINES

Peter Elson looks back at Liverpool's great shipping lines, the people and the buildings

RRP £4.99

NEW ONLY £2.50

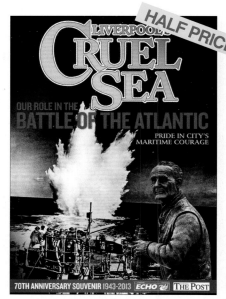

HALF PRICE

NOW £2.50
LIVERPOOL'S CRUEL SEA

Marking the 70th anniversary of the Battle of the Atlantic – the city's own secret story

A CITY ON THE MOVE

Join us on a nostalgic journey from the Overhead Railway to the steam train